Computerised Payroll Practice Set
Using MYOB AccountRight

Expert Level

This expert level computerised accounting practice set is for students who need to practice payroll exercises of MYOB AccountRight, students can process four weekly pay runs of Richmond Papers Pty Ltd and can create payroll reports.

It covers the following topics.

- Setting Up a New Accounting System
- Wages
- Taxes
- Entitlements
- Superannuation
- Payroll Reports

Syed Tirmizi
Certified Advisor

ISBN 978-0-9945988-2-0

9 780994 598820 >

For enquiries, please contact **syed.tirmizi@mail.com**

Part A
Practice Set

This page is blank.

Instructions

You have recently been appointed as a Payroll Officer at Richmond Papers Pty Ltd, a new business dealing in printing and publishing. Your responsibilities are to input payroll data accurately and process weekly pay run of all employees. The company started trading on 1st April 2016.

You are required to complete the following tasks in the order given.

Task 1   Setup a New Accounting System

A.   Create the following data file in MYOB AccountRight Plus for Richmond Papers Pty Ltd.

Company Details and General Payroll Information

Company Name	Richmond Papers Pty Ltd
ABN	46 995 263 632
Address	23 High Street, Richmond VIC 3121
Phone Number	03 9876 5432
Financial Year	01-Jul-15 to 30-Jun-16
Conversion Month	June
Accounts List	Start with an accounts list provided by MYOB
Industry	Retail
Payroll Year	01-Jul-15 to 30-Jun-16
Full Work Week Hours	38

B.   Set up all employees on the system together with their provided payroll details.

C.   Print or save Employee Employment Details report before moving to the next section.

Task 2   Process Pay Run of Week 1

Payment Date	4th April 2016
Pay Period	1st April to 3rd April 2016

Employee Name	Pay Basis	Hours	1.5x Hours	2x Hours
Paul Nguyen	Salary		2	2
Andrew Lee	Salary		2	2
Sue Malcolm	Hourly	7.5		
Laura Smith	Salary		2	
Joanne Peters	Hourly	8.5		
David Wilson	Hourly	7.5		

▪   Print or save Payroll Advice report of the above run.

Task 3   Process Pay Run of Week 2

Payment Date   11th April 2016
Pay Period   4th April to 10th April 2016

Employee Name	Pay Basis	Hours	1.5x Hours	2x Hours
Paul Nguyen	Salary			
Andrew Lee	Salary		2	
Sue Malcolm	Hourly	8.5		
Laura Smith	Salary		2	2
Joanne Peters	Hourly	16		2
David Wilson	Hourly	8	2	2

- Print or save Payroll Advice report of the above run.

Task 4   Process Pay Run of Week 3

Payment Date   18th April 2016
Pay Period   11th April to 17th April 2016

Employee Name	Pay Basis	Hours	1.5x Hours	2x Hours
Paul Nguyen	Salary		2	2
Andrew Lee	Salary			
Sue Malcolm	Hourly	9	2	
Laura Smith	Salary			2
Joanne Peters	Hourly	8	2	
David Wilson	Hourly	15.5		2

- Print or save Payroll Advice report of the above run.

Task 5   Process Pay Run of Week 4

Payment Date   25th April 2016
Pay Period   18th April to 24th April 2016

Employee Name	Pay Basis	Hours	1.5x Hours	2x Hours
Paul Nguyen	Salary			
Andrew Lee	Salary		2	2
Sue Malcolm	Hourly	15		
Laura Smith	Salary		2	
Joanne Peters	Hourly	9		2
David Wilson	Hourly	8		

- Print or save Payroll Advice report of the above run.

Employee # 1

Profile

Card ID	NGU001
Last Name	Nguyen
First Name	Paul
Address	87 East Avenue
City	Box Hill
State and Postcode	VIC 3128
Phone	03 9400 1111

Payroll Details

Personal Details

Date of Birth	5/07/1979
Gender	Male
Start Date	1/04/2016
Employment Status	Full Time

Wages

Pay Basis	Salary
Annual Salary	$38,000
Pay Frequency	Weekly
Weekly Hours	38
Annual Leave Pay	✓
Base Salary	✓
Overtime (1.5x)	✓
Overtime (2x)	✓
Personal Leave Pay	✓

Superannuation

Superannuation Fund	Spectrum
Membership Number	025695
Superannuation Guarantee	✓

Entitlements

Annual Leave Accrual	✓
Personal Leave Accrual	✓

Taxes

TFN	111 222 333
Tax Table	Tax Free Threshold
PAYG Withholding	✓

Payment Details

Payment Method	Electronic
Bank Account Name	Paul Nguyen
BSB Number	123-456
Bank Account Number	111111111

Employee # 2

Profile

Card ID	LEE001
Last Name	Lee
First Name	Andrew
Address	2/259 Cheddar Road
City	Camberwell
State and Postcode	VIC 3124
Phone	03 9400 2222

Payroll Details

Personal Details

Date of Birth	10/12/1983
Gender	Male
Start Date	1/04/2016
Employment Status	Part Time

Wages

Pay Basis	Salary
Annual Salary	$18,000
Pay Frequency	Weekly
Weekly Hours	19
Annual Leave Pay	✓
Base Salary	✓
Overtime (1.5x)	✓
Overtime (2x)	✓
Personal Leave Pay	✓

Superannuation

Superannuation Fund	Spectrum
Membership Number	590312
Superannuation Guarantee	✓

Entitlements

Annual Leave Accrual	✓
Personal Leave Accrual	✓

Taxes

TFN	222 333 444
Tax Table	Tax Free Threshold
PAYG Withholding	✓

Payment Details

Payment Method	Electronic
Bank Account Name	Andrew Lee
BSB Number	123-456
Bank Account Number	222222222

Employee # 3

Profile

Card ID	MAL001
Last Name	Malcolm
First Name	Sue
Address	5/456 North Road
City	Chadstone
State and Postcode	VIC 3148
Phone	03 9400 3333

Payroll Details

Personal Details

Date of Birth	16/02/1981
Gender	Female
Start Date	1/04/2016
Employment Status	Casual

Wages

Pay Basis	Hourly
Hourly Rate	$20.00
Pay Frequency	Weekly
Weekly Hours	7.5
Annual Leave Pay	
Base Hourly	✓
Overtime (1.5x)	✓
Overtime (2x)	✓
Personal Leave Pay	

Superannuation

Superannuation Fund	Spectrum
Membership Number	109252
Superannuation Guarantee	✓

Entitlements

Annual Leave Accrual	
Personal Leave Accrual	

Taxes

TFN	333 444 555
Tax Table	Tax Free Threshold
PAYG Withholding	✓

Payment Details

Payment Method	Electronic
Bank Account Name	Sue Malcolm
BSB Number	123-456
Bank Account Number	333333333

Employee # 4

Profile

Card ID	SMI001
Last Name	Smith
First Name	Laura
Address	34 Abbott Road
City	St Albans
State and Postcode	VIC 3021
Phone	03 9400 4444

Payroll Details

Personal Details

Date of Birth	19/09/1987
Gender	Female
Start Date	1/04/2016
Employment Status	Part Time

Wages

Pay Basis	Salary
Annual Salary	$9,000
Pay Frequency	Weekly
Weekly Hours	10
Annual Leave Pay	✓
Base Salary	✓
Overtime (1.5x)	✓
Overtime (2x)	✓
Personal Leave Pay	✓

Superannuation

Superannuation Fund	Spectrum
Membership Number	213156
Superannuation Guarantee	✓

Entitlements

Annual Leave Accrual	✓
Personal Leave Accrual	✓

Taxes

TFN	444 555 666
Tax Table	Tax Free Threshold
PAYG Withholding	✓

Payment Details

Payment Method	Electronic
Bank Account Name	Laura Smith
BSB Number	123-456
Bank Account Number	444444444

Employee # 5

Profile

Card ID	PET001
Last Name	Peters
First Name	Joanne
Address	59 Melrose Drive
City	Oakleigh
State and Postcode	VIC 3166
Phone	03 9400 5555

Payroll Details

Personal Details

Date of Birth	16/10/1991
Gender	Female
Start Date	1/04/2016
Employment Status	Casual

Wages

Pay Basis	Hourly
Hourly Rate	$20.00
Pay Frequency	Weekly
Weekly Hours	7.5
Annual Leave Pay	
Base Hourly	✓
Overtime (1.5x)	✓
Overtime (2x)	✓
Personal Leave Pay	

Superannuation

Superannuation Fund	Spectrum
Membership Number	658429
Superannuation Guarantee	✓

Entitlements

Annual Leave Accrual	
Personal Leave Accrual	

Taxes

TFN	555 666 777
Tax Table	Tax Free Threshold
PAYG Withholding	✓

Payment Details

Payment Method	Electronic
Bank Account Name	Joanne Peters
BSB Number	123-456
Bank Account Number	555555555

Employee # 6

Profile

Card ID	WIL001
Last Name	Wilson
First Name	David
Address	68 Richmond Road
City	Richmond
State and Postcode	VIC 3121
Phone	03 9400 6666

Payroll Details

Personal Details

Date of Birth	23/02/1980
Gender	Male
Start Date	1/04/2016
Employment Status	Casual

Wages

Pay Basis	Hourly
Hourly Rate	$20
Pay Frequency	Weekly
Weekly Hours	7.5
Annual Leave Pay	
Base Hourly	✓
Overtime (1.5x)	✓
Overtime (2x)	✓
Personal Leave Pay	

Superannuation

Superannuation Fund	Spectrum
Membership Number	547339
Superannuation Guarantee	✓

Entitlements

Annual Leave Accrual	
Personal Leave Accrual	

Taxes

TFN	666 777 888
Tax Table	Tax Free Threshold
PAYG Withholding	✓

Payment Details

Payment Method	Electronic
Bank Account Name	David Wilson
BSB Number	123-456
Bank Account Number	666666666

Part B

Solutions

This page is blank.

Employee Employment Details

Richmond Papers Pty Ltd
23 High Street
Richmond
VIC 3121
ABN: 46 995 263 632

Name:	Paul Nguyen	Status:	Active
Card ID:	NGU001	Gender:	Male
Address 1:	87 East Avenue Box Hill VIC 3128	Date Of Birth:	5/07/1979
		Address 1 Phone#1:	03 9400 1111
Tax File Number:	111 222 333	Start Date:	1/04/2016
Employment Basis:	Individual	Payment Method:	Electronic
Employment Category:	Permanent	Pay Frequency:	Weekly
Employment Status:	FullTime	Hours in pay period:	38.000
Pay Basis:	Salary	Hourly Rate:	$19.23
Tax Scale:	Tax Free Threshold	Annual Salary:	$38,000.00
Total Rebates:	$0.00	Extra Tax:	$0.00
Superannuation Fund:	Spectrum Super		
Employee Membership #:	025695		

Page 1 of 6

Employee Employment Details

Richmond Papers Pty Ltd
23 High Street
Richmond
VIC 3121

ABN: 46 995 263 632

Name:	Andrew Lee	Status:	Active
Card ID:	LEE001	Gender:	Male
Address 1:	2/259 Cheddar Road Camberwell VIC 3124	Date Of Birth:	10/12/1983
		Address 1 Phone#1:	03 9400 2222
Tax File Number:	222 333 444	Start Date:	1/04/2016
Employment Basis:	Individual	Payment Method:	Electronic
Employment Category:	Permanent	Pay Frequency:	Weekly
Employment Status:	PartTime	Hours in pay period:	19.000
Pay Basis:	Salary	Hourly Rate:	$18.22
Tax Scale:	Tax Free Threshold	Annual Salary:	$18,000.00
Total Rebates:	$0.00	Extra Tax:	$0.00
Superannuation Fund:	Spectrum Super		
Employee Membership #:	590312		

Page 2 of 6

Employee Employment Details

Richmond Papers Pty Ltd
23 High Street
Richmond
VIC 3121

ABN: 46 995 263 632

Name:	Sue Malcolm	Status:	Active
Card ID:	MAL001	Gender:	Female
Address 1:	4/456 North Road Chadstone VIC 3148	Date Of Birth:	16/02/1981
		Address 1 Phone#1:	03 9400 3333
Tax File Number:	333 444 555	Start Date:	1/04/2016
Employment Basis:	Individual	Payment Method:	Electronic
Employment Category:	Permanent	Pay Frequency:	Weekly
Employment Status:	Casual	Hours in pay period:	7.500
Pay Basis:	Hourly	Hourly Rate:	$20.00
Tax Scale:	Tax Free Threshold	Annual Salary:	$7,800.00
Total Rebates:	$0.00	Extra Tax:	$0.00
Superannuation Fund:	Spectrum Super		
Employee Membership #:	109252		

Employee Employment Details

Richmond Papers Pty Ltd
23 High Street
Richmond
VIC 3121

ABN: 46 995 263 632

Name:	Laura Smith	Status:	Active
Card ID:	SMI001	Gender:	Female
Address 1:	34 Abbott Road St Albans VIC 3021	Date Of Birth:	19/09/1987
		Address 1 Phone#1:	03 9400 4444
Tax File Number:	444 555 666	Start Date:	1/04/2016
Employment Basis:	Individual	Payment Method:	Electronic
Employment Category:	Permanent	Pay Frequency:	Weekly
Employment Status:	PartTime	Hours in pay period:	10.000
Pay Basis:	Salary	Hourly Rate:	$17.31
Tax Scale:	Tax Free Threshold	Annual Salary:	$9,000.00
Total Rebates:	$0.00	Extra Tax:	$0.00
Superannuation Fund:	Spectrum Super		
Employee Membership #:	213156		

Page 4 of 6

Employee Employment Details

Richmond Papers Pty Ltd
23 High Street
Richmond
VIC 3121

ABN: 46 995 263 632

Name:	Joanne Peters	Status:	Active
Card ID:	PET001	Gender:	Female
Address 1:	59 Melrose Drive Oakleigh VIC 3166	Date Of Birth:	16/10/1991
		Address 1 Phone#1:	03 9400 5555
Tax File Number:	555 666 777	Start Date:	1/04/2016
Employment Basis:	Individual	Payment Method:	Electronic
Employment Category:	Permanent	Pay Frequency:	Weekly
Employment Status:	Casual	Hours in pay period:	7.500
Pay Basis:	Hourly	Hourly Rate:	$20.00
Tax Scale:	Tax Free Threshold	Annual Salary:	$7,800.00
Total Rebates:	$0.00	Extra Tax:	$0.00
Superannuation Fund:	Spectrum Super		
Employee Membership #:	658429		

Richmond Papers Pty Ltd
23 High Street
Richmond
VIC 3121

ABN: 46 995 263 632

Employee Employment Details

Name:	David Wilson	Status:	Active
Card ID:	WIL001	Gender:	Male
Address 1:	68 Richmond Road Richmond VIC 3121	Date Of Birth:	23/02/1980
		Address 1 Phone#1:	03 9400 6666
Tax File Number:	666 777 888	Start Date:	1/04/2016
Employment Basis:	Individual	Payment Method:	Electronic
Employment Category:	Permanent	Pay Frequency:	Weekly
Employment Status:	Casual	Hours in pay period:	7.500
Pay Basis:	Hourly	Hourly Rate:	$20.00
Tax Scale:	Tax Free Threshold	Annual Salary:	$7,800.00
Total Rebates:	$0.00	Extra Tax:	$0.00
Superannuation Fund:	Spectrum Super		
Employee Membership #:	547339		

Payroll Advice

04-Apr-16 To 04-Apr-16

Richmond Papers Pty Ltd
23 High Street
Richmond
VIC 3121

ABN: 46 995 263 632

| **Richmond Papers Pty Ltd** | | **Cheque No: 1** |
| A.B.N.: 46 995 263 632 | | **Payment Date: 04-Apr-16** |

Andrew Lee	Card ID:LEE001	Gross Pay: $473.68
Pay Frequency: Weekly		Net Pay: $443.68
Pay Period: 01-Apr-16 to 03-Apr-16		
Annual Salary: $18,000.00		
Hourly Rate: $18.22		
Employment Classification:		
Superannuation Fund:	Spectrum Super	

Description	Hours	Calc. Rate	Amount	YTD	Type
Overtime (1.5x)	2	$27.33	$54.66	$54.66	Wages
Overtime (2x)	2	$36.435	$72.87	$72.87	Wages
Base Salary			$346.15	$346.15	Wages
PAYG Withholding			-$30.00	($30.00)	Tax
Annual Leave Accrual	0.308			0.31	Entitlements

| **Richmond Papers Pty Ltd** | | **Cheque No: 2** |
| A.B.N.: 46 995 263 632 | | **Payment Date: 04-Apr-16** |

Sue Malcolm	Card ID:MAL001	Gross Pay: $150.00
Pay Frequency: Weekly		Net Pay: $150.00
Pay Period: 01-Apr-16 to 03-Apr-16		
Annual Salary: $7,800.00		
Hourly Rate: $20.00		
Employment Classification:		
Superannuation Fund:	Spectrum Super	

Description	Hours	Calc. Rate	Amount	YTD	Type
Base Hourly	7.5	$20	$150.00	$150.00	Wages

Page 1 of 3

Payroll Advice

04-Apr-16 To 04-Apr-16

Richmond Papers Pty Ltd
23 High Street
Richmond
VIC 3121

ABN: 46 995 263 632

Richmond Papers Pty Ltd		**Cheque No: 3**
A.B.N.: 46 995 263 632		**Payment Date: 04-Apr-16**

Paul Nguyen		**Card ID:NGU001**	**Gross Pay: $865.38**
Pay Frequency:	Weekly		**Net Pay: $729.38**
Pay Period:	01-Apr-16 to 03-Apr-16		
Annual Salary:	$38,000.00		
Hourly Rate:	$19.23		
Employment Classification:			
Superannuation Fund:		Spectrum Super	

Description	Hours	Calc. Rate	Amount	YTD	Type
Overtime (1.5x)	2	$28.845	$57.69	$57.69	Wages
Overtime (2x)	2	$38.46	$76.92	$76.92	Wages
Base Salary			$730.77	$730.77	Wages
PAYG Withholding			-$136.00	($136.00)	Tax
Annual Leave Accrual	0.308			0.31	Entitlements
Superannuation Guarantee			$69.42	$69.42	Superannuation Expenses

Richmond Papers Pty Ltd		**Cheque No: 4**
A.B.N.: 46 995 263 632		**Payment Date: 04-Apr-16**

Joanne Peters		**Card ID:PET001**	**Gross Pay: $170.00**
Pay Frequency:	Weekly		**Net Pay: $170.00**
Pay Period:	01-Apr-16 to 03-Apr-16		
Annual Salary:	$7,800.00		
Hourly Rate:	$20.00		
Employment Classification:			
Superannuation Fund:		Spectrum Super	

Description	Hours	Calc. Rate	Amount	YTD	Type
Base Hourly	8.5	$20	$170.00	$170.00	Wages

Page 2 of 3

Payroll Advice

04-Apr-16 To 04-Apr-16

Richmond Papers Pty Ltd
23 High Street
Richmond
VIC 3121
ABN: 46 995 263 632

Richmond Papers Pty Ltd
A.B.N.:   46 995 263 632

Cheque No: 5
Payment Date: 04-Apr-16

Laura Smith   Card ID:SMI001   Gross Pay: $225.00
Pay Frequency: Weekly   Net Pay: $225.00
Pay Period: 01-Apr-16 to 03-Apr-16
Annual Salary: $9,000.00
Hourly Rate: $17.31
Employment Classification:
Superannuation Fund: Spectrum Super

Description	Hours	Calc. Rate	Amount	YTD	Type
Overtime (1.5x)	2	$25.96	$51.92	$51.92	Wages
Base Salary			$173.08	$173.08	Wages
Annual Leave Accrual	0.154			0.15	Entitlements

Richmond Papers Pty Ltd
A.B.N.:   46 995 263 632

Cheque No: 6
Payment Date: 04-Apr-16

David Wilson   Card ID:WIL001   Gross Pay: $150.00
Pay Frequency: Weekly   Net Pay: $150.00
Pay Period: 01-Apr-16 to 03-Apr-16
Annual Salary: $7,800.00
Hourly Rate: $20.00
Employment Classification:
Superannuation Fund: Spectrum Super

Description	Hours	Calc. Rate	Amount	YTD	Type
Base Hourly	7.5	$20	$150.00	$150.00	Wages

Page 3 of 3

Richmond Papers Pty Ltd
23 High Street
Richmond
VIC 3121

Payroll Advice

11-Apr-16 To 11-Apr-16

ABN: 46 995 263 632

Richmond Papers Pty Ltd	**Cheque No: 7**
A.B.N.: 46 995 263 632	**Payment Date: 11-Apr-16**

Andrew Lee	Card ID:LEE001	**Gross Pay: $400.81**
Pay Frequency: Weekly		**Net Pay: $391.81**
Pay Period: 04-Apr-16 to 10-Apr-16		
Annual Salary: $18,000.00		
Hourly Rate: $18.22		
Employment Classification:		
Superannuation Fund:	Spectrum Super	

Description	Hours	Calc. Rate	Amount	YTD	Type
Overtime (1.5x)	2	$27.33	$54.66	$109.32	Wages
Base Salary			$346.15	$692.30	Wages
PAYG Withholding			-$9.00	($39.00)	Tax
Annual Leave Accrual	0.154			0.46	Entitlements
Superannuation Guarantee			$65.77	$65.77	Superannuation Expenses

Richmond Papers Pty Ltd	**Cheque No: 8**
A.B.N.: 46 995 263 632	**Payment Date: 11-Apr-16**

Sue Malcolm	Card ID:MAL001	**Gross Pay: $170.00**
Pay Frequency: Weekly		**Net Pay: $170.00**
Pay Period: 04-Apr-16 to 10-Apr-16		
Annual Salary: $7,800.00		
Hourly Rate: $20.00		
Employment Classification:		
Superannuation Fund:	Spectrum Super	

Description	Hours	Calc. Rate	Amount	YTD	Type
Base Hourly	8.5	$20	$170.00	$320.00	Wages

Page 1 of 3

Richmond Papers Pty Ltd
23 High Street
Richmond
VIC 3121

Payroll Advice

11-Apr-16 To 11-Apr-16

ABN: 46 995 263 632

Richmond Papers Pty Ltd		**Cheque No: 9**
A.B.N.: 46 995 263 632		**Payment Date: 11-Apr-16**

Paul Nguyen	**Card ID:NGU001**	**Gross Pay: $730.77**
Pay Frequency: Weekly		**Net Pay: $641.77**
Pay Period: 04-Apr-16 to 10-Apr-16		
Annual Salary: $38,000.00		
Hourly Rate: $19.23		
Employment Classification:		
Superannuation Fund:	Spectrum Super	

Description	Hours	Calc. Rate	Amount	YTD	Type
Base Salary			$730.77	$1,461.54	Wages
PAYG Withholding			-$89.00	($225.00)	Tax
Superannuation Guarantee			$69.43	$138.85	Superannuation Expenses

Richmond Papers Pty Ltd		**Cheque No: 10**
A.B.N.: 46 995 263 632		**Payment Date: 11-Apr-16**

Joanne Peters	**Card ID:PET001**	**Gross Pay: $400.00**
Pay Frequency: Weekly		**Net Pay: $391.00**
Pay Period: 04-Apr-16 to 10-Apr-16		
Annual Salary: $7,800.00		
Hourly Rate: $20.00		
Employment Classification:		
Superannuation Fund:	Spectrum Super	

Description	Hours	Calc. Rate	Amount	YTD	Type
Base Hourly	16	$20	$320.00	$490.00	Wages
Overtime (2x)	2	$40	$80.00	$80.00	Wages
PAYG Withholding			-$9.00	($9.00)	Tax
Superannuation Guarantee			$46.55	$46.55	Superannuation Expenses

Page 2 of 3

Payroll Advice

11-Apr-16 To 11-Apr-16

Richmond Papers Pty Ltd
23 High Street
Richmond
VIC 3121

ABN: 46 995 263 632

Richmond Papers Pty Ltd		**Cheque No: 11**
A.B.N.:　　　　46 995 263 632		**Payment Date: 11-Apr-16**

Laura Smith		Card ID:SMI001	**Gross Pay: $294.23**
Pay Frequency:	Weekly		**Net Pay: $294.23**
Pay Period:	04-Apr-16 to 10-Apr-16		
Annual Salary:	$9,000.00		
Hourly Rate:	$17.31		
Employment Classification:			
Superannuation Fund:		Spectrum Super	

Description	Hours	Calc. Rate	Amount	YTD	Type
Overtime (1.5x)	2	$25.96	$51.92	$103.84	Wages
Overtime (2x)	2	$34.615	$69.23	$69.23	Wages
Base Salary			$173.08	$346.16	Wages
Annual Leave Accrual	0.308			0.46	Entitlements

Richmond Papers Pty Ltd			**Cheque No: 12**
A.B.N.:　　　　46 995 263 632			**Payment Date: 11-Apr-16**

David Wilson		Card ID:WIL001	**Gross Pay: $300.00**
Pay Frequency:	Weekly		**Net Pay: $300.00**
Pay Period:	04-Apr-16 to 10-Apr-16		
Annual Salary:	$7,800.00		
Hourly Rate:	$20.00		
Employment Classification:			
Superannuation Fund:		Spectrum Super	

Description	Hours	Calc. Rate	Amount	YTD	Type
Base Hourly	8	$20	$160.00	$310.00	Wages
Overtime (1.5x)	2	$30	$60.00	$60.00	Wages
Overtime (2x)	2	$40	$80.00	$80.00	Wages

Page 3 of 3

Payroll Advice

18-Apr-16 To 18-Apr-16

Richmond Papers Pty Ltd
23 High Street
Richmond
VIC 3121

ABN: 46 995 263 632

Richmond Papers Pty Ltd
A.B.N.:   46 995 263 632

Cheque No: 13
Payment Date: 18-Apr-16

Andrew Lee   Card ID:LEE001   Gross Pay: $346.15
Pay Frequency: Weekly   Net Pay: $346.15
Pay Period: 11-Apr-16 to 17-Apr-16
Annual Salary: $18,000.00
Hourly Rate: $18.22
Employment Classification:
Superannuation Fund: Spectrum Super

Description	Hours	Calc. Rate	Amount	YTD	Type
Base Salary			$346.15	$1,038.45	Wages
Superannuation Guarantee			$32.88	$98.65	Superannuation Expenses

---

Richmond Papers Pty Ltd
A.B.N.:   46 995 263 632

Cheque No: 14
Payment Date: 18-Apr-16

Sue Malcolm   Card ID:MAL001   Gross Pay: $240.00
Pay Frequency: Weekly   Net Pay: $240.00
Pay Period: 11-Apr-16 to 17-Apr-16
Annual Salary: $7,800.00
Hourly Rate: $20.00
Employment Classification:
Superannuation Fund: Spectrum Super

Description	Hours	Calc. Rate	Amount	YTD	Type
Base Hourly	9	$20	$180.00	$500.00	Wages
Overtime (1.5x)	2	$30	$60.00	$60.00	Wages
Superannuation Guarantee			$47.50	$47.50	Superannuation Expenses

---

Richmond Papers Pty Ltd
A.B.N.:   46 995 263 632

Cheque No: 15
Payment Date: 18-Apr-16

Paul Nguyen   Card ID:NGU001   Gross Pay: $865.38
Pay Frequency: Weekly   Net Pay: $729.38
Pay Period: 11-Apr-16 to 17-Apr-16
Annual Salary: $38,000.00
Hourly Rate: $19.23
Employment Classification:
Superannuation Fund: Spectrum Super

Page 1 of 3

Richmond Papers Pty Ltd
23 High Street
Richmond
VIC 3121

Payroll Advice

18-Apr-16 To 18-Apr-16

ABN: 46 995 263 632

Description	Hours	Calc. Rate	Amount	YTD	Type
Overtime (1.5x)	2	$28.845	$57.69	$115.38	Wages
Overtime (2x)	2	$38.46	$76.92	$153.84	Wages
Base Salary			$730.77	$2,192.31	Wages
PAYG Withholding			-$136.00	($361.00)	Tax
Annual Leave Accrual	0.308			0.62	Entitlements
Superannuation Guarantee			$69.42	$208.27	Superannuation Expenses

---

Richmond Papers Pty Ltd
A.B.N.: 46 995 263 632

Cheque No: 16
Payment Date: 18-Apr-16

Joanne Peters
Pay Frequency: Weekly
Pay Period: 11-Apr-16 to 17-Apr-16
Annual Salary: $7,800.00
Hourly Rate: $20.00
Employment Classification:
Superannuation Fund: Spectrum Super

Card ID:PET001

Gross Pay: $220.00
Net Pay: $220.00

Description	Hours	Calc. Rate	Amount	YTD	Type
Base Hourly	8	$20	$160.00	$650.00	Wages
Overtime (1.5x)	2	$30	$60.00	$60.00	Wages
Superannuation Guarantee			$15.20	$61.75	Superannuation Expenses

---

Richmond Papers Pty Ltd
A.B.N.: 46 995 263 632

Cheque No: 17
Payment Date: 18-Apr-16

Laura Smith
Pay Frequency: Weekly
Pay Period: 11-Apr-16 to 17-Apr-16
Annual Salary: $9,000.00
Hourly Rate: $17.31
Employment Classification:
Superannuation Fund: Spectrum Super

Card ID:SMI001

Gross Pay: $242.31
Net Pay: $242.31

Description	Hours	Calc. Rate	Amount	YTD	Type
Overtime (2x)	2	$34.615	$69.23	$138.46	Wages
Base Salary			$173.08	$519.24	Wages
Annual Leave Accrual	0.154			0.62	Entitlements
Superannuation Guarantee			$49.33	$49.33	Superannuation Expenses

---

Page 2 of 3

Payroll Advice

18-Apr-16 To 18-Apr-16

Richmond Papers Pty Ltd
23 High Street
Richmond
VIC 3121

ABN: 46 995 263 632

Richmond Papers Pty Ltd	**Cheque No: 18**
A.B.N.: 46 995 263 632	**Payment Date: 18-Apr-16**

David Wilson	Card ID:WIL001	Gross Pay: $390.00
Pay Frequency: Weekly		Net Pay: $383.00
Pay Period: 11-Apr-16 to 17-Apr-16		
Annual Salary: $7,800.00		
Hourly Rate: $20.00		
Employment Classification:		
Superannuation Fund:	Spectrum Super	

Description	Hours	Calc. Rate	Amount	YTD	Type
Base Hourly	15.5	$20	$310.00	$620.00	Wages
Overtime (2x)	2	$40	$80.00	$160.00	Wages
PAYG Withholding			-$7.00	($7.00)	Tax
Superannuation Guarantee			$58.90	$58.90	Superannuation Expenses

Payroll Advice

Richmond Papers Pty Ltd
23 High Street
Richmond
VIC 3121

ABN: 46 995 263 632

25-Apr-16 To 25-Apr-16

Richmond Papers Pty Ltd
A.B.N.: 46 995 263 632

Cheque No: 19
Payment Date: 25-Apr-16

Andrew Lee

Card ID:LEE001

Gross Pay: $473.68
Net Pay: $443.68

Pay Frequency:	Weekly
Pay Period:	18-Apr-16 to 24-Apr-16
Annual Salary:	$18,000.00
Hourly Rate:	$18.22
Employment Classification:	
Superannuation Fund:	Spectrum Super

Description	Hours	Calc. Rate	Amount	YTD	Type
Overtime (1.5x)	2	$27.33	$54.66	$163.98	Wages
Overtime (2x)	2	$36.435	$72.87	$145.74	Wages
Base Salary			$346.15	$1,384.60	Wages
PAYG Withholding			-$30.00	($69.00)	Tax
Annual Leave Accrual	0.308			0.77	Entitlements
Superannuation Guarantee			$32.89	$131.54	Superannuation Expenses

---

Richmond Papers Pty Ltd
A.B.N.: 46 995 263 632

Cheque No: 20
Payment Date: 25-Apr-16

Sue Malcolm

Card ID:MAL001

Gross Pay: $300.00
Net Pay: $300.00

Pay Frequency:	Weekly
Pay Period:	18-Apr-16 to 24-Apr-16
Annual Salary:	$7,800.00
Hourly Rate:	$20.00
Employment Classification:	
Superannuation Fund:	Spectrum Super

Description	Hours	Calc. Rate	Amount	YTD	Type
Base Hourly	15	$20	$300.00	$800.00	Wages
Superannuation Guarantee			$28.50	$76.00	Superannuation Expenses

---

Page 1 of 3

Payroll Advice

25-Apr-16 To 25-Apr-16

Richmond Papers Pty Ltd
23 High Street
Richmond
VIC 3121
ABN: 46 995 263 632

| **Richmond Papers Pty Ltd** | **Cheque No: 21** |
| A.B.N.: 46 995 263 632 | **Payment Date: 25-Apr-16** |

Paul Nguyen   Card ID:NGU001

			Gross Pay: $730.77
Pay Frequency:	Weekly		Net Pay: $641.77
Pay Period:	18-Apr-16 to 24-Apr-16		
Annual Salary:	$38,000.00		
Hourly Rate:	$19.23		
Employment Classification:			
Superannuation Fund:		Spectrum Super	

Description	Hours	Calc. Rate	Amount	YTD	Type
Base Salary			$730.77	$2,923.08	Wages
PAYG Withholding			-$89.00	($450.00)	Tax
Superannuation Guarantee			$69.42	$277.69	Superannuation Expenses

---

| **Richmond Papers Pty Ltd** | **Cheque No: 22** |
| A.B.N.: 46 995 263 632 | **Payment Date: 25-Apr-16** |

Joanne Peters   Card ID:PET001

			Gross Pay: $150.00
Pay Frequency:	Weekly		Net Pay: $150.00
Pay Period:	18-Apr-16 to 24-Apr-16		
Annual Salary:	$7,800.00		
Hourly Rate:	$20.00		
Employment Classification:			
Superannuation Fund:		Spectrum Super	

Description	Hours	Calc. Rate	Amount	YTD	Type
Base Hourly	7.5	$20	$150.00	$800.00	Wages
Superannuation Guarantee			$14.25	$76.00	Superannuation Expenses

---

| **Richmond Papers Pty Ltd** | **Cheque No: 23** |
| A.B.N.: 46 995 263 632 | **Payment Date: 25-Apr-16** |

Laura Smith   Card ID:SMI001

			Gross Pay: $242.31
Pay Frequency:	Weekly		Net Pay: $242.31
Pay Period:	18-Apr-16 to 24-Apr-16		
Annual Salary:	$9,000.00		
Hourly Rate:	$17.31		
Employment Classification:			
Superannuation Fund:		Spectrum Super	

Page 2 of 3

Payroll Advice

Richmond Papers Pty Ltd
23 High Street
Richmond
VIC 3121

25-Apr-16 To 25-Apr-16

ABN: 46 995 263 632

Description	Hours	Calc. Rate	Amount	YTD	Type
Overtime (2x)	2	$34.615	$69.23	$207.69	Wages
Base Salary			$173.08	$692.32	Wages
Annual Leave Accrual	0.154			0.77	Entitlements
Superannuation Guarantee			$16.44	$65.77	Superannuation Expenses

Richmond Papers Pty Ltd
A.B.N.:   46 995 263 632

Cheque No: 24
Payment Date: 25-Apr-16

David Wilson
Card ID:WIL001

Gross Pay: $160.00
Net Pay: $160.00

Pay Frequency:	**Weekly**
Pay Period:	**18-Apr-16 to 24-Apr-16**
Annual Salary:	**$7,800.00**
Hourly Rate:	**$20.00**
Employment Classification:	
Superannuation Fund:	**Spectrum Super**

Description	Hours	Calc. Rate	Amount	YTD	Type
Base Hourly	8	$20	$160.00	$780.00	Wages
Superannuation Guarantee			$15.20	$74.10	Superannuation Expenses

Page 3 of 3